SUMMARY
of David Grann's
KILLERS OF THE FLOWER MOON

The Osage Murders and the Birth of the FBI

by SUMOREADS

TABLE OF CONTENTS

EXECUTIVE SUMMARY

David Grann's *Killers of the Flower Moon: The Osage Murders and the Birth of the FBI* recounts how Tom White, an FBI investigator, straddles the divide between the old Wild West-style law enforcement and its new Progressivism movement predicated on rational, evidence-based, scientific investigation. In Osage County, Oklahoma, Tom White is tasked with solving the Osage murders case, in which twenty-four Osage individuals were suspected of being murdered, but nobody could figure out who or why these killings were happening. The case was four years old, and the Bureau of Investigation—still in its early years, and later transformed into the FBI—was under a lot of pressure to solve it, especially with a new, ambitious director named J. Edgar Hoover at the helm. He would go on to preside as director of the FBI (and Bureau of Investigation) for forty-eight years. At the time however, Hoover was anxious to solve this troubling case and used its success as a springboard toward launching the Federal Bureau of Investigation's genesis myth.

Tom White leads a team of undercover agents into Osage County, carefully eliminating suspects and probing witnesses until he discovers that William K. Hale, the "King of the Osage Hills," is pulling countless local strings to deviate the investigation away from him. What follows is a breathtaking account of a true story filled with corruption and crime—a raw story of how law enforcement can bring out the rawness and depth of (in)humanity.

CHRONICLE I: THE MARKED WOMAN

Chapter 1: The Vanishing

Mollie Burkhart of the Native American Osage Tribe in Gray Horse Oklahoma was worried about the disappearance of her sister Anna. Though she was known to leave for days on end to party in the nearby Oklahoma City and Kansas City clubs, the discovery of another member of the Osage tribe's dead body with execution style bullets in his head only a couple days earlier was reason for concern. Indeed a few days later, Anna's body was found decomposing in a ravine.

Chapter 2: An Act of God or Man

As a coroner's inquest composed of ordinary citizens began to determine whether Anna died at the hands of god or men, it was concluded that she had been shot in the back of the head. While Mollie prepared her sister's funeral, the county sheriff, 58-year-old Harve M. Freas was called to pursue those responsible for the murder.

Chapter 3: King of the Osage Hills

As the murders of Anna Brown and Charles Whitehorn made a sensation, authorities didn't seem to care much. Instead, Mollie turned to Ernest's uncle William Hale who had been an advocate for law and order in the county and was reserve deputy sheriff in Fairfax. One day, a man who had been arrested in Kansas claimed he had been paid by Oda Brown

(Anna's ex-husband) $8000 to murder Anna. He was arrested but subsequently released due to insufficient evidence. By July 1921, a couple of months after Anna's murder, the justice of the peace had closed both inquiries when Lizzie (Mollie and Anna's mother) died of a mysterious illness that doctors couldn't diagnose. Mollie's brother-in-law became convinced she'd been poisoned.

Chapter 4: Underground Reservation

The story of how the Osage tribe came to inhabit the parcel of land in Oklahoma that happened to be sitting on top of a large oil field can be traced back to the 17th century. At the time, the Osage had laid claim to much of central North America in today's Missouri, Kansas and Oklahoma in a territory that stretched all the way to the Rockies. Gradually throughout the 18th century they were forced off their land as settlers massacred them, pillaged their graves and forced them to sell their lands at minimal prices. As their numbers shrunk considerably due to the forced migrations and diseases brought by the settlers, they finally moved to Wild Horse in Oklahoma. Having witnessed the land rushes that ravaged the Cherokee territory, they sent a talented young lawyer to Washington to negotiate their settlement in Wild Horse. In the 1906 Allotment Act that consecrated the negotiations process, a phrase was included that would later ensure the Osage's wealth. It stated: "That the oil, gas, coal, or other minerals covered by the lands… are hereby reserved to the Osage Tribe."

Chapter 5: The Devil's Disciples

As official investigators continued to be indifferent to the murder of Anna and the possible poisoning of her mother, Mollie issued a $2000 reward for any information leading to the arrest of those responsible. She also hired a series of private investigators who seemed to quickly reach an impasse. When another series of murders shook the county, the Osage turned to Barney McBride, a wealthy white oilman with contacts in Washington to try to have the government open a federal investigation. As he went up to Washington he received a telegram from an associate warning him to "be careful." The next day he was found dead with 26 stab wounds and a crushed skull.

Chapter 6: Million Dollar Elm

The oil wealth of Osage County brought all the wealthiest oil magnates of the United States to congregate four times a year for the land auctions. Fortunes were made and lost in these tense meetings that witnessed the rise of the oil industry. The oil magnates of the 20th century were amongst the most powerful men in the history of the country, arguably more so than the steel and railroad barons of the 19th century. In 1920, Sinclair, Marland, and other oilmen financed the victory of Warren Harding for president and though the influence of private interest in politics was not yet widely known, these oilmen undeniably defined the course of American history.

Chapter 7: This Thing of Darkness

In February 1923, six months after the murder of the oilman McBride, 42-year-old Osage Henry Roan was found in his car shot in the back of the head. As a climate of terror took hold of the Osage County community and all the neighborhood watchdogs were found poisoned, Bill and Rita Smith decided to move to a house in Fairfax, leaving all their belongings behind. However, when they refused to sell their property in Wild Horse, a bomb was placed under their home killing them both. After Oklahoma Governor Jack C. Watson was impeached and replaced by W.W Vaughan—who discovered crucial information about the murder spree—he was himself murdered before being able to reveal his discoveries. By this time, the official Osage Reign of Terror death toll had climbed to twenty-four and finally the government sent federal investigators to Osage County.

CHRONICLE II:
THE EVIDENCE MAN

Chapter 8: Department of Easy Virtue

In the early stages of the Bureau's recent creation, it did not hold nearly as many cases as it does today, dealing mainly in various small crimes, and holding no power to arrest people. Tom White joined the Bureau in 1917, serving previously as a Texas Ranger, and even then—nine years after its creation—agents were not allowed to carry guns. In the early 1920s, the director, William Burns, was crooked and hired individuals who followed his example—the agency was then known as the Department of Easy Virtue. J. Edgar Hoover was his replacement, one who would bring reforms, but also "commit egregious abuses of power" (p.108). The Osage murders case, which was a case concerning 24 dead Osage in Oklahoma City, including a few agents, was an example of that. Hoover strove to make sure that the press never heard of the bureau's failures in the investigation, but there were many complaints, leading to a tenuous link in Hoover's hold on power. He appointed Tom White to solve the dangerous Osage case, knowing that if he failed, the bureau would be in a precarious position.

Chapter 9: The Undercover Boys

White took over the Oklahoma City field office in July 1925. Four years had gone by since the start of the case, making the task of solving it all the more arduous. All of the murders seemed random except for the fact that rich Osage Indians were being targeted, and three of the victims were family related. Complicating matters even further was the fact that corruption was rampant in the local law enforcement of the area. White decided to make himself the public face of the investigation, while coordinating with a secret team of undercover agents.

Chapter 10: Eliminating the Impossible

The undercover agents began the task of presenting their covers to the people of Osage County: two ranchers, an insurance salesman, and a Native American medicine man. White didn't know where to start, since the evidence kept from the crime scenes was virtually all gone, except for the skull of Anna Brown. There was no exit wound in the skull, and no bullet had been found during the autopsy, which means that someone had taken it. Someone had clearly altered the crime scene, but White had no idea who. White then set about corroborating everyone's alibis, quickly setting aside many suspects whose alibis checked out. An informant called 'Morrison' seemed to show that Rose Osage, who was a suspect who had apparently confessed to another woman, did not commit Anna's murder, and other evidence pointed the same way too. It soon became clear however that someone was manufacturing evidence to point to Rose.

Chapter 11: The Third Man

Hoover was getting nervous about the slow progress of the case, and started poring over the reports with greater tenacity. He believed that Necia Kenny, married to an Osage man, might hold the key to the case. She had told agents that an attorney named A.W. Comstock, who, incidentally, had also criticized the bureau, was probably part of the conspiracy. Though Comstock would also appear to be helping at times, he would suspiciously ask for access to FBI files so as to "secure critical evidence" (p. 127). Another suspect in Anna's murders was Bryan Burkhart whose alibi was cracked by a pair of key witnesses who saw him in the car with Anna before she died, along with—possibly—a third man.

Chapter 12: A Wilderness of Mirrors

White began to suspect that there was a mole inside his investigative team. Some private eyes even tried to expose Morrison as the informant that he was, sending him off to jail on trumped-up charges. One private eye named Pike, who was hired by William Hale in 1921 to solve the murder case, apparently knew who the third man was—but was determined to be paid for his knowledge.

Chapter 13: A Hangman's Son

This chapter focuses on Tom White, and his upbringing in Texas as the sheriff's son. Grann demonstrates that Tom White often wondered about the question of justice and the law, especially considering how primitive investigative tactics were back then. Relating the time he had witnessed his first execution, Tom White offered up that it was precisely because of those executions that he opposed what he called "judicial homicide" (p. 143). Grann then goes on to describe how White became a lawman, and how he learned the tools of his trade.

Chapter 14: Dying Words

White suspected that Bill Smith, Mollie Burkhart's brother-in-law, had uncovered the secrets that Ernest and Bryan were seemingly hiding. It was highly possible, and equally troubling, that he had been killed for what he knew. Smith apparently stated that he only had two enemies: William Hale, the King of the Osage Hills and Ernest Burkhart. It became more and more clear to White that everything connected with the Osage was hopelessly rank with corruption, leading back to "the crooked guardians and administrators of Osage estates [who] were typically among the most prominent white citizens" (p. 154).

Chapter 15: The Hidden Face

Through White's undercover operative working as an insurance salesman, he discovered many shady insurance dealings—including the fact that Hale owned Roan's $25,000 life-insurance policy, which he was then able to collect when Henry Roan was found dead with a bullet in his head. Local lawmen never opened any investigation into Hale, and even tried to push Roan's murder onto Roy Bunch, a man who had been having an affair with Roan's wife. White also realized that Hale's scheme did not stop at the life-insurance policy, but that he was actually after Roan's headright—something that, under the law, could not be bought or sold, but only inherited. It just so happened that many of the Osage headrights, which were immensely valuable, were being passed on by inheritance to Mollie Burkhart, Ernest Burkhart's wife. White therefore suspected that the Osage murders were a cunning and planned series of murders, orchestrated by William Hale to gain various headrights that amounted to a fortune.

Chapter 16: For the Betterment of the Bureau

With White in charge, it seemed as though the investigation was processing much more rapidly than it ever had—but White was still unable to gather anything more than circumstantial evidence to back up his theories. As a result, Hoover was growing more and more impatient. He was a man who advocated for Progressivism, a movement that endorsed scientific procedure and organization. On the one hand, it allowed for true reform within the corruption of law enforcement agencies, yet on the other, the Progressives who were championed and mirrored by Hoover "held deep prejudices against immigrants and blacks and were so convinced of their own virtuous authority that they disdained democratic procedures" (p. 166). Additionally, while Hoover was treating the bureau like a business, with its constant employee turnover, White believed that the agency would be better served by having local and regional agents familiar with the area. Ultimately, however, White soon came to fall in step with Hoover's policies, even becoming "almost indistinguishable from one of Hoover's college boys" (p. 170).

Chapter 17: The Quick-Draw Artist, the Yegg, and the Soup Man

Hoover was not the only one pressuring White. The head of the investigation saw that the members of the Osage community were terrified, and had no faith whatsoever in the Justice Department. They were fleeing the county in large numbers. White understood that "prejudiced and corrupt white citizens would not implicate one of their own in the killing of American Indians" (p. 171-172). He pivoted to a new strategy of gaining witnesses from the outlaws of the Osage Hills, many of whom had information about the killings, and could be leveraged into talking. Dick Gregg was one such individual, and claimed that Hale had offered to pay him to kill Bill Smith and his wife—an assignment that he refused to undertake. As White investigated the names that Gregg and other criminals gave to corroborate such an account, he discovered that most of them were dead.

Chapter 18: The State of the Game

In October 1925, White received a tip from a prisoner at the state penitentiary called Burt Lawson who claimed to have information on the Osage murders. Lawson knew that Smith was having an affair with his wife and detested him, but still refused to blow up their house when Hale offered him the job. After landing in jail for robbery, Hale told Lawson that he would need lawyers, otherwise he would be going to prison for a long time, and he promised he could give him the money for it. Hale then snuck Lawson out of jail so that he could light the fuse for the nitroglycerin. After Lawson had done the job, Hale smuggled him back into the jail, giving him the perfect alibi. White was ecstatic, and set off corroborating the loose ends that remained. Nonetheless, he had his key witness. His main worry now was the fate of Mollie Burkhart, who was the sole inheritor of all the inheritances, as well as Comstock, whom he now believed was actively helping the investigation. As a result, White believed that he could no longer afford to wait, and on January 4, 1926, he issued the arrest warrants for Hale and Ernest Burkhart. The latter was soon found, but Hale could not be captured, until he suddenly appeared at the sheriff's office to turn himself in. Hale maintained his innocence, and White was certain that, of the two, only Ernest Burkhart would break. It soon became evident that Lawson had been lying to have his sentence shortened, but White was able to find another witness: Blackie Thompson. He was unreliable, and Hoover would surely not have signed off on using him, but it was White's last card.

At last, however, Ernest Burkhart pronounced himself ready to confess: Hale had indeed orchestrated everything. After gathering all of the testimonies needed to charge Hale with the murders, White was hoping that Hale would confess as well. Unfortunately for him, Hale was determined to fight the charges until the end—leading to a "bitter, sensational legal battle [...] that would be debated in the U.S. Supreme Court and would nearly destroy [White's] career" (p. 195).

Chapter 19: A Traitor To His Blood

White had not yet been able to connect Hale to all 24 Osage murders, or to the deaths of others also connected. When the news of White's apparent success in tying Hale to the murders came out, it caused a sensational uproar that was part horror and part fascination. However, White knew that the saga of the investigation was not close to over: Hale still held incredible influence over local lawmen and judiciaries. For this reason, White decided to try Hale in the federal courts for the Roan murder investigation—the only murder case that applied. As the trial came closer, it was clear that Hale's men were attempting to sway the case, through intoxication of the jury, or even assassination of key witnesses. Unfortunately for White, Hale managed to find a way to swing the case back into the state court, where he had much more sway. White's prosecutors appealed for the Supreme Court, but that ruling would take months. In addition, when Ernest Burkhart's turn to testify came, he decided to recant his confession—leaving the prosecution with no hard evidence to present for Hale's crimes. Even worse, Hale turned the case around and accused the FBI of electrically abusing Ernest Burkhart and himself so as to gain a forced confession. In the end, Ernest Burkhart was unable to live with the burden of lying, entered a plea of guilty, and was sentenced to life in prison.

Chapter 20: So Help You God

Hale tried multiple times to break out some of the outlaws, like Blackie Thompson, who would be testifying against him in his and Ramsey's trial. White was also wary of jury and witness tampering, which Hale had already attempted, leading to the dismissal of the first batch of jurors. All of these elements didn't even take into account the question on everyone's mind, as one Osage member stated bluntly:

"The question for them to decide is whether a white man killing an Osage is murder—or merely cruelty to animals" (p. 215).

This time, however, Ernest Burkhart did testify against Hale and divulged everything he knew. Nonetheless, it all added up to a hung jury, with evidence of conspiracy to obstruct justice, which meant a retrial. In the second trial, both Hale and Ramsey were found guilty of first-degree murder, and sentenced to life in prison. Hoover took most of the credit for the operation's success and crafted an origin story to prop up the FBI's legend. White and his team of operatives were only credited by the Osage Tribal Council, who recognized the tremendous work they had done. Finally, Tom White left the FBI and became warden of Leavenworth Prison, where Hale and Ramsey would join him—but as inmates.

Chapter 21: The Hot House

Inside Leavenworth Prison, also nicknamed the Hot House because of absurdly high temperatures that could rise up to 115 degrees, White came across many of the outlaws that had passed through his life. Even so, White soon earned a reputation for being strict but fair, much like his father had been. Hale never admitted to the murders he had orchestrated. He steadfastly maintained his innocence, and constantly attempted to escape through bribes and contacts outside the prison. On December 11, 1931, White was taken hostage by seven armed convicts, of which Hale was not part of, and who escaped into the wilderness. In a later struggle with the escaped convicts, Hale was shot in the arm, which would forever dangle uselessly as a result, but managed to save the lives of two young children in the process. None of the convicts got away safely, and three of them died. The Osage murders were the bureau's springboard into relevance, and launched Hoover into stardom, but his abuses of power would not become public until after his death in 1972. Hoover's agents, including Tom White, died in relative obscurity, often in poverty, with little thanks or recognition of the way they had put their lives on the line time and time again.

CHRONICLE III:
THE REPORTER

Chapter 22: Ghostlands

After having spent 10 years of a life sentence in Prison, Ernest Burkart was released only to be caught stealing from an Osage house and imprisoned once more until his final release in 1959. Pardoned from his Oklahoma banishment he spent the years until his death in 1986 living in a small trailer outside Osage County. Hale was released in 1947 after having spent twenty years in prison and died in 1962 in an Arizona nursing home.

Chapter 23: A Case Not Closed

After Hale and his conspirators were found guilty and given life sentences for the murders of the Reign of Terror, the authorities insisted that all guilty parties had been discovered and punished and the cases of the twenty-four official murders were closed. However, Hale had not been connected to all of the murders and when a relative of W.W Vaughan continued to investigate his death, he received an anonymous threat warning him to stop investigating if he did not wish to end up like W.W Vaughan. As the author David Grann researched the book it became increasingly clear that a man by the name of H.G Burt had been involved in the killing, but the truth will never be known for certain.

Chapter 24: Standing In Two Worlds

As Grann went to a May 2013 showing of the Osage ballet Wahzhazhe, he contemplated the message of the ballet that depicts the collision of the two worlds the Osage straddled. As he digs deeper into the unsolved or unofficial murders of other Osages that were unconnected to Hale, he realizes the secret history of the Reign of terror: Hale's evil was not an anomaly. One side of the Osage's world was almost systematically out to kill them and rob them of their wealth. Undertakers, doctors, police officers and citizens from every walk of life had conspired to cover up these Osage murders.

Chapter 25: The Lost Manuscript

As 2014 oil regulations stopped oil drilling on the Osage reservation for the first time in a hundred years, the Italian oil conglomerate Enel built scores of windmills across the Osage territory. In a lawsuit in which the federal government represented the Osage Nation, it was claimed that these windmill fields violated the terms of the 1906 Allotment Act by requiring the excavation of minerals. While the Osage lost the trial, plans for a second field were already being put in place. In addition, there was also a discovery of another murder for an oil headright in 1918 which contradicted the official narrative of the four years that spanned the Reign of Terror from Anna Brown's murder in 1921 to January 1926 when Hale was arrested.

Chapter 26: Blood Cries Out

As Grann continues to research the period of the Reign of Terror, he finds many indications that contradict the official narrative that it merely spanned the four-year period from Anna Brown's murder in 1921 to Hale's arrest in January 1926. The more he digs into records and testimonies from descendants of the Osage living in the early 20th century, the more it becomes evident that the murder spree was much more widespread than officially believed. The extremely high death rates amongst Osages with guardians having the possibility upon the death of their wards to manage their estates, is particularly indicative that there was systematic murder of the Osage for their wealth and for access to their oil headrights. So many murders were so well concealed or so poorly documented that many families of victims are now condemned to never have a final resolution to these sordid affairs.

KEY TAKEAWAYS

Key Takeaway: In the 1920's the Osage tribe were considered the wealthiest people per capita in the world

The entire tribe had been driven from their land in Kansas and resettled in Gray Horse, Oklahoma, only to discover that they were sitting on top of one of the greatest oil deposits ever discovered. In the year 1923 alone, the tribe earned more than $30 million (equal to more than $400 million in today's currency).

Key Takeaway: Police stations only emerged in the mid-nineteenth century, prior to which ordinary citizens were responsible for justice

Following the American Revolution, people were afraid of the potential repression stemming from an organized and official criminal justice system, and it was only after the growth of industrial cities in the mid-nineteenth century, coupled with the spread of urban riots that accompanied it, that police departments began to emerge in the United States.

***Key Takeaway: Over the two decades following
President Jefferson's purchase of Louisiana
from the French, the Osage were forced to
abandon a hundred million acres of their
ancestral land***

In 1803, President Thomas Jefferson bought the Osage
dominated territory of Louisiana from the French. He
promised the Osage tribal leaders friendship, but within four
years had forced them to abandon their territory between the
Missouri and Arkansas rivers. Gradually, the Osage were
continuously removed from their lands until they found
refuge in a 50-by-125-mile parcel of land in today's
southeastern Kansas. In 1870, they were once more forced out
of their land, which they agreed to sell for $1.25 per acre and
settled in Wild Horse.

***Key Takeaway: Toward the end of the 19th
century, the U.S policy toward tribes changed
from one of containment to one of forced
assimilation***

The government that owed the Osage tribe annual payments
for the sale of their land in Kansas refused to make the
payments unless the Osage men took up farming. Even then,
considering that these "savages" knew not how to use money,
they only payed them in clothes and rations. The Osage
reservation in Wild horse was also divided into individual
allotments in order to end the communal life style of the tribe
and turn each family into property owners—making it easier
for the property to be bought off them. Finally, the Osage

children were obliged to attend catholic schools where they were taught English, Catholicism and "civilized ways."

Key Takeaway: During much of the 19th and early 20th centuries, private detectives compensated for the shortcomings of the sheriff and police departments

These private eyes compensated for the underfunded, incompetent and corrupt official alternatives by surreptitiously uncovering people's secrets. "To detect" was derived from the Latin "to unroof," referring to the legend that the devil allowed his minions to peer into houses, thus giving private detectives the nickname "devil's disciples." The first private American detective agency was founded in 1850 by Allan Pinkerton.

Key Takeaway: Many Osage did not have access to their own funds and were legally required to have a guardian

The U.S federal government, deeming the Osage incapable of managing their own finances, obliged any American Indian considered "incompetent" by the Department of Interior to find a guardian who had to approve any spending. The level of competence was essentially based on the amount of Indian blood in the property owner. A full-blooded Indian Osage was systematically forced to have a white guardian. Furthermore, the Osage were also restricted to spending a few thousand dollars annually and thus often had to resort to asking for loans despite having plentiful amounts of finances in their trust funds.

Key Takeaway: The FBI was created in 1908 by President Theodore Roosevelt

It was created as a national police force, something that many people and legislators at the time were unsure about. This then led Roosevelt's attorney general to push the creation through without legislative approval.

Key Takeaway: The Teapot Dome Scandal revealed how corrupt the agency was

When Congress decided to investigate the Justice Department, Burns had the congressmen's phones tapped, made sure they were shadowed, their offices broken into, and generally led a large operation of obstruction of justice.

Key Takeaway: William Hale was protecting Bryan Burkhart by paying Pike to create an alibi

William Hale, who was described as the "seeming paragon of law and order" (p. 136), did not hire Pike to solve the investigation; he hired him so as to make sure that his nephews Bryan and Ernest Burkhart, along with their parents, were never under suspicion. This then raised the troubling question of whether William Hale was only protecting the family, or was he part of some "intricate, nefarious design?" (p. 136).

Key Takeaway: One Osage widow was robbed of her money

In a heinous, yet typical, example of the exploitation taking place in the county, an Osage widow with two children, including a baby, was stripped of all her money, and left with "not a bed nor a chair nor food in the house" (p.156). As a result, the widow's baby got sick and quickly died, even after the mother had pleaded with the guardian to return her money to give him food and proper medical care.

Key Takeaway: Rose Osage was rumored to be Anna's murderer

Rose Osage and Joe Allen, (her boyfriend at the time and her husband since) had given the same alibi, even though Rose had apparently previously confessed to a Kaw Native American that she was the murderer. A suspicious looking stain that looked like blood had also been found in the backseat of Anna's car. Rose and Joe's stories were almost verbatim, which was also suspicious to the investigators. Nonetheless, the Kaw woman soon admitted that she had been forced to fabricate the confession story, which cleared Rose of suspicion.

Key Takeaway: Mollie Burkhart was being deprived of insulin for her diabetes

Mollie Burkhart was suffering from diabetes and was also growing increasingly worried that she would be poisoned. The town's doctors, including the Shoun brothers, whom White suspected of being under Hale's influence, had been injecting her with a substance that did not improve her diabetes, but actively worsened it. She was being slowly and deliberately poisoned. As further proof of the poison that was slowly accumulating in her (so as to escape detection), when Mollie Burkhart was removed from the custody of Ernest Burkhart and Hale, she immediately started regaining her health.

Key Takeaway: The Osage Murders Investigation launched the power of the FBI

Hoover made sure that everyone, especially Congress, realized the potential of the FBI. A series of highly public crimes such as the kidnapping of Charles Lindbergh's baby, as well as the Kansas City Massacre, helped to solidify his arguments. As a result, Congress passed a series of New Deal reforms that included a federal criminal code, as well as more responsibility to the bureau: agents could now make arrests and carry firearms. Grann also notes that "Hoover ensured that the identity of the bureau was indistinguishable from his own" (p. 232).

Key Takeaway: There is little oil left in the oil fields of Osage County

An auction for Osage oil leases held in Tulsa in 2012 saw three leases sold for a total value of $15,000, a fraction of their worth in the peak years of Osage wealth. Little remains today of the petroleum companies, large oil fields, outlaws and moonshine bars of Osage County. Pawhuska with its 3600 inhabitants is still the capital of Osage Nation: the twenty thousand inhabitant autonomous nation with its own elected government and newly ratified 2006 constitution. The Osages have found a new source of revenue in the territory's seven casinos that, along with their $380 million settlement against the federal government, fund their government education and health-care programs.

Key Takeaway: The Osage tribe had some prominent figures in American history

The Osage have produced many of the United States' greatest ballerinas—among them Maria Tallchief, considered to be America's first major prima ballerina. Clarence Leonard Tinker was the first Native American to become major general. He died in a plane crash in World War II.

EDITORIAL REVIEW

David Grann's *Killers of the Flower Moon: The Osage Murders and the Birth of the FBI* recounts how Tom White, an FBI investigator, straddles the divide between the old Wild West-style law enforcement and its new Progressivism movement predicated on rational, evidence-based, scientific investigation. The narrative is a masterfully woven tale of murder on a scale unlike anything many have ever seen or heard of. Grann deftly weaves the origins of the FBI and the commanding personality of its director, J. Edgar Hoover, into the suspenseful chronology of Tom White's investigation into the Osage murders. It is not easy to transport readers into the heart of Oklahoma while tracking Hoover's desires and ambitions, but Grann manages to pull us in—perhaps precisely because the murders are so sensationalist, and also because Hoover is such an iconic figure.

However, aside from the main players, some of the individuals are hard to remember and follow along with. To his credit, however, Grann does make sure to remind the reader what precise role each character has in this book. Periodically, he reminds us that Ernest Burkhart is William K. Hale's nephew—a crucially important fact that allows the reader to understand many of the forces acting behind the scenes. As the narrative unfolds, many of the pieces that seemed mysterious or unknown start to fall into place for the reader, testifying to Grann's fabulous handle on suspense. He divulges neither too much nor too little, and constantly leads the reader down narrow paths that may seem promising, only to be revealed as dead-ends. He keeps you on your toes. There are not many non-fiction books that can boast such an attribute.

KEY PLAYERS

J. Edgar Hoover: Director of the FBI.

Tom White: Agent in charge of the Osage murders investigation.

William K. Hale: The so-called "King of the Osage Hills"—was later convicted of first-degree murder in the investigation.

Ernest Burkhart: Nephew of William Hale. Conspired with his uncle to murder several Osage for their wealth.

Byron Burkhart: Nephew of William Hale, and brother to Ernest Burkhart.

Mollie Burkhart: Wife of Ernest Burkhart. Was almost a victim of the deadly conspiracy.

ABOUT THE AUTHOR

David Grann is a staff writer at *The New Yorker* who has won honors for outstanding journalism including a George Polk Award and the Samuel Johnson Prize. He is also a bestselling author, having written *The Lost City of Z*, chosen by *The Washington Post* and *The New York Times* as one of the best books of the year, as well as *The Devil and Sherlock Holmes*. His works have been translated into twenty-five languages.

THE END

If you enjoyed this summary, please leave an honest review on Amazon.com…it'd mean a lot to us.

If you haven't already, we encourage you to purchase a copy of the original book.

71197865R00020

Made in the USA
Lexington, KY
18 November 2017